# The Ice Storm

**Kieran Kiley**

There is ice on the leaves.

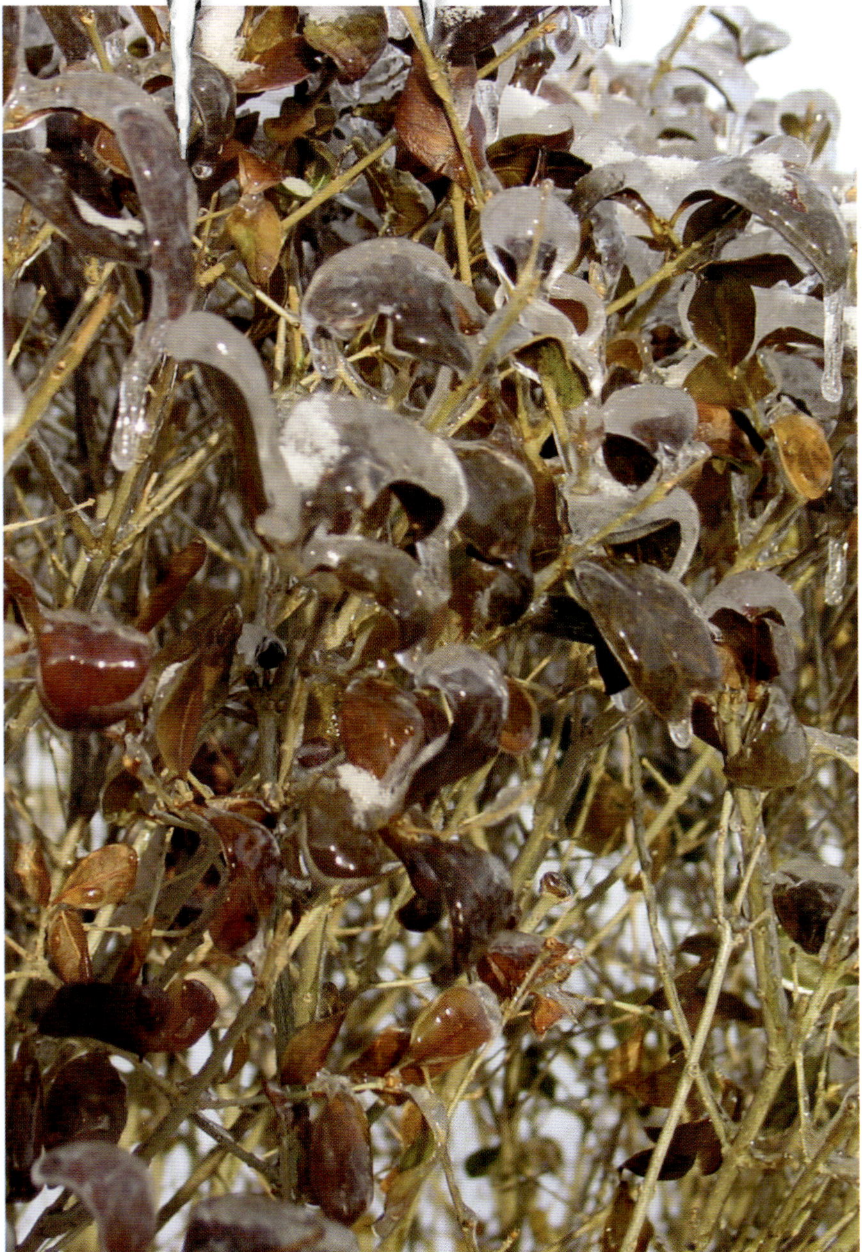

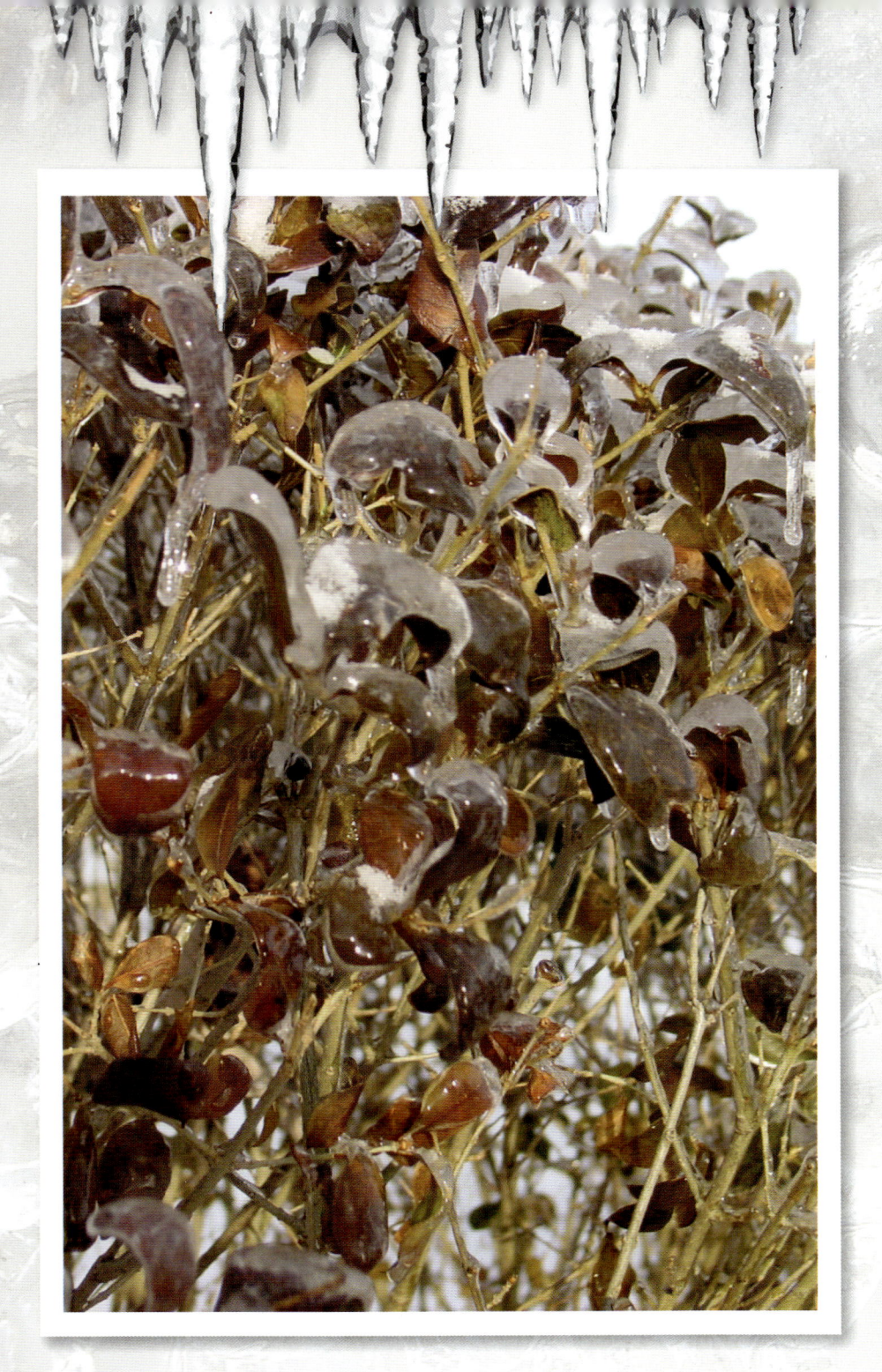

There is ice on the steps.

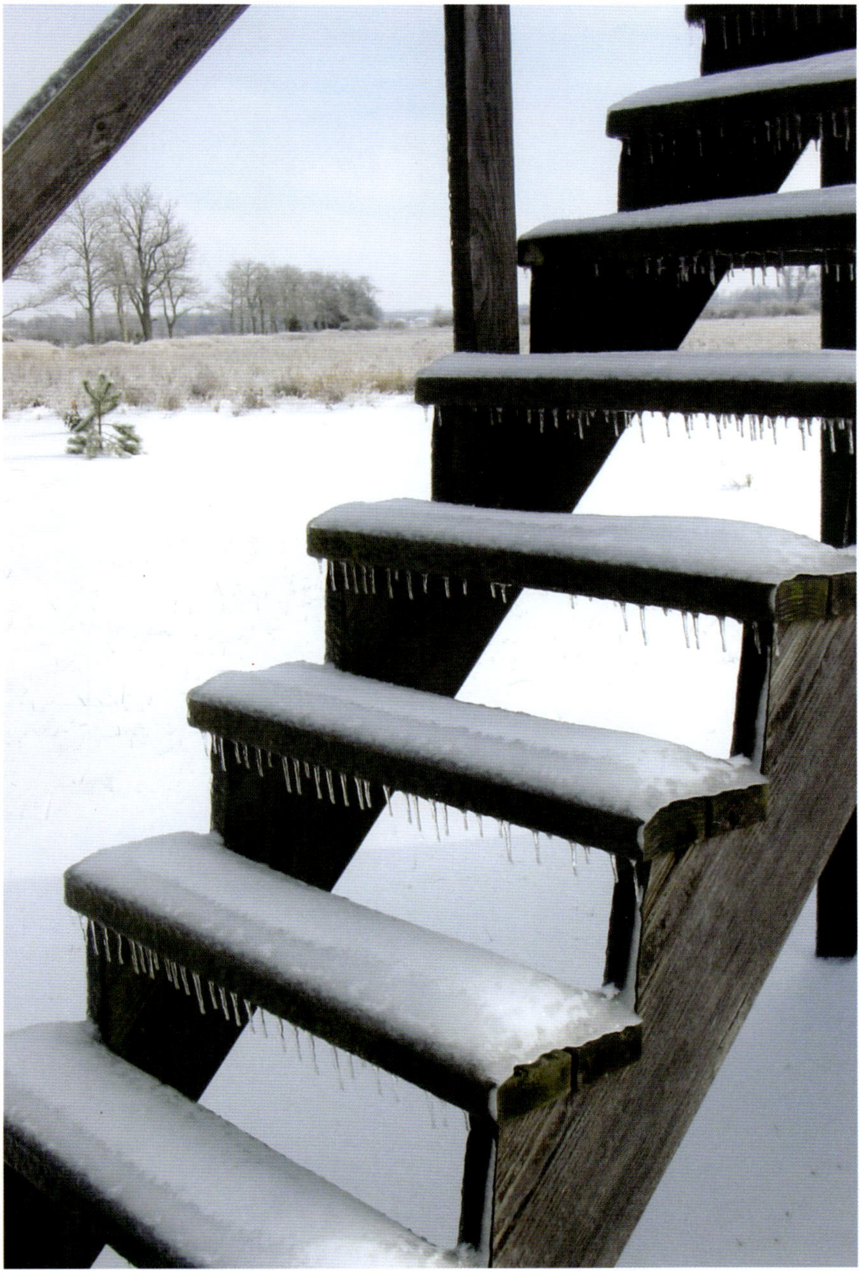

There is ice on the tree.

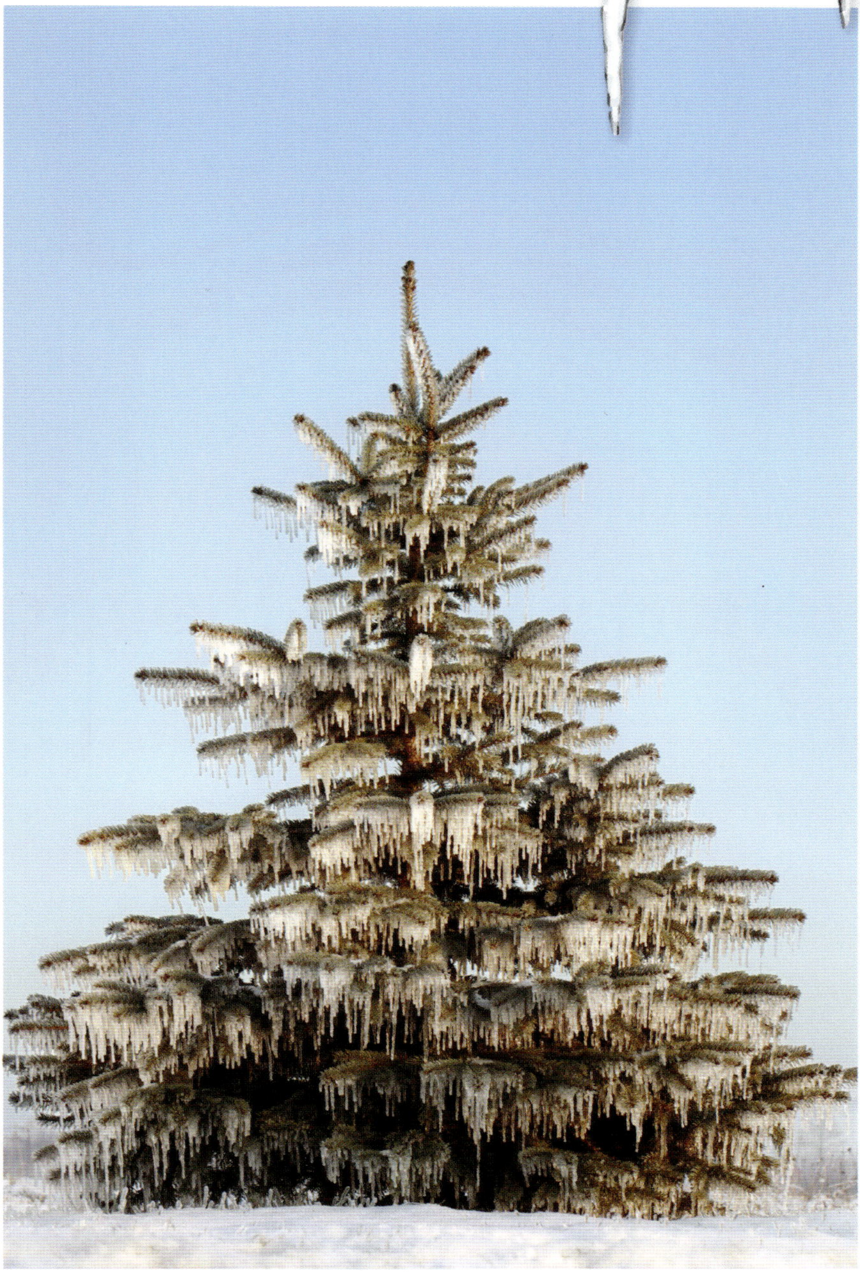

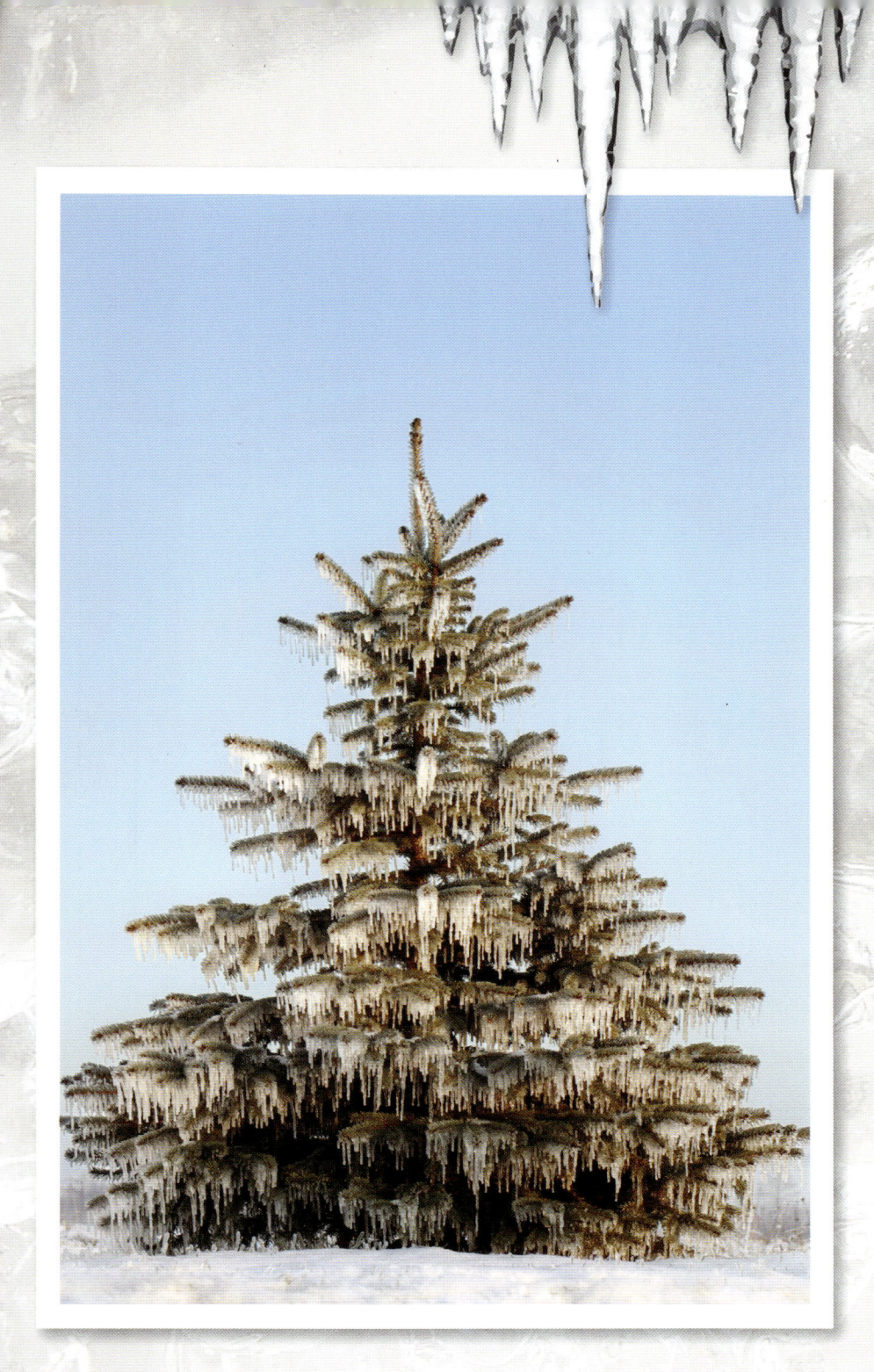

There is ice on the roof.

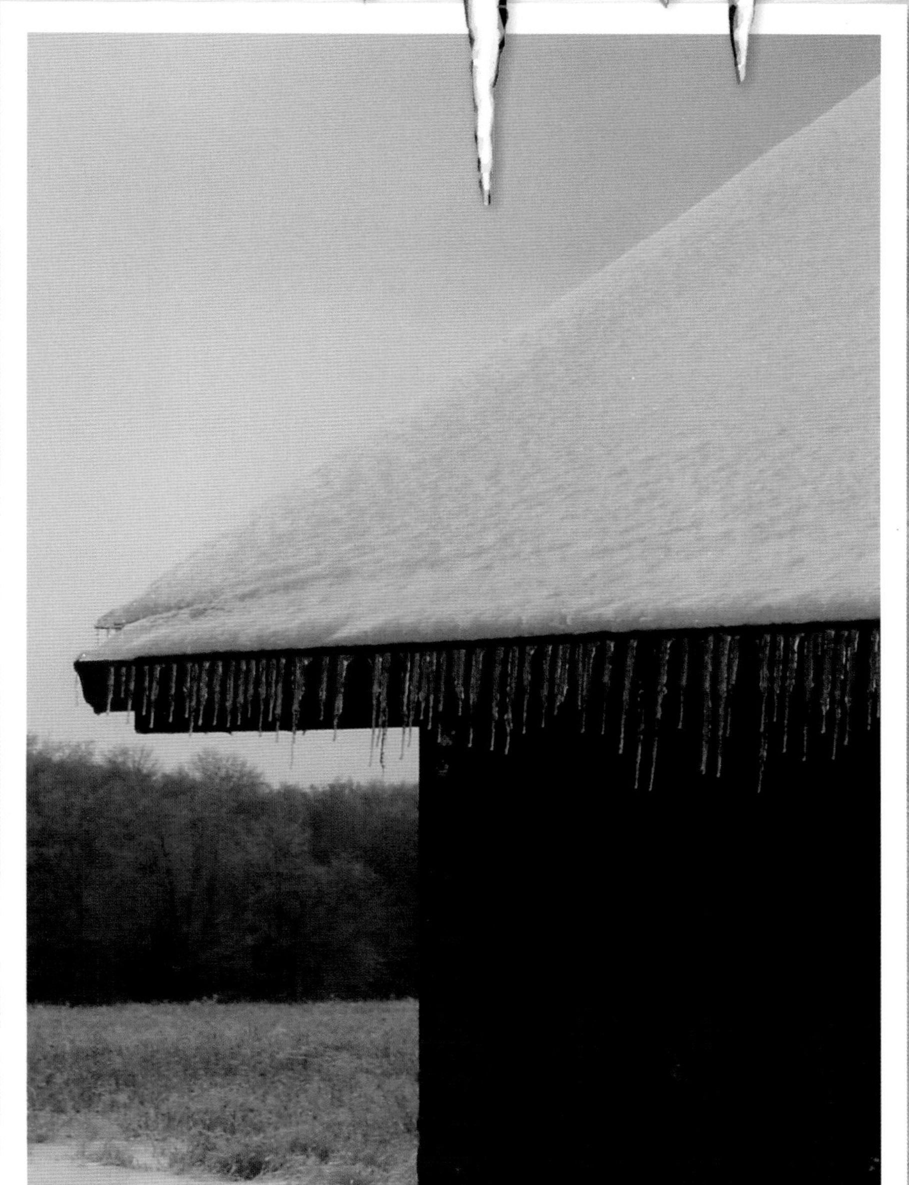

There is ice on the berries.

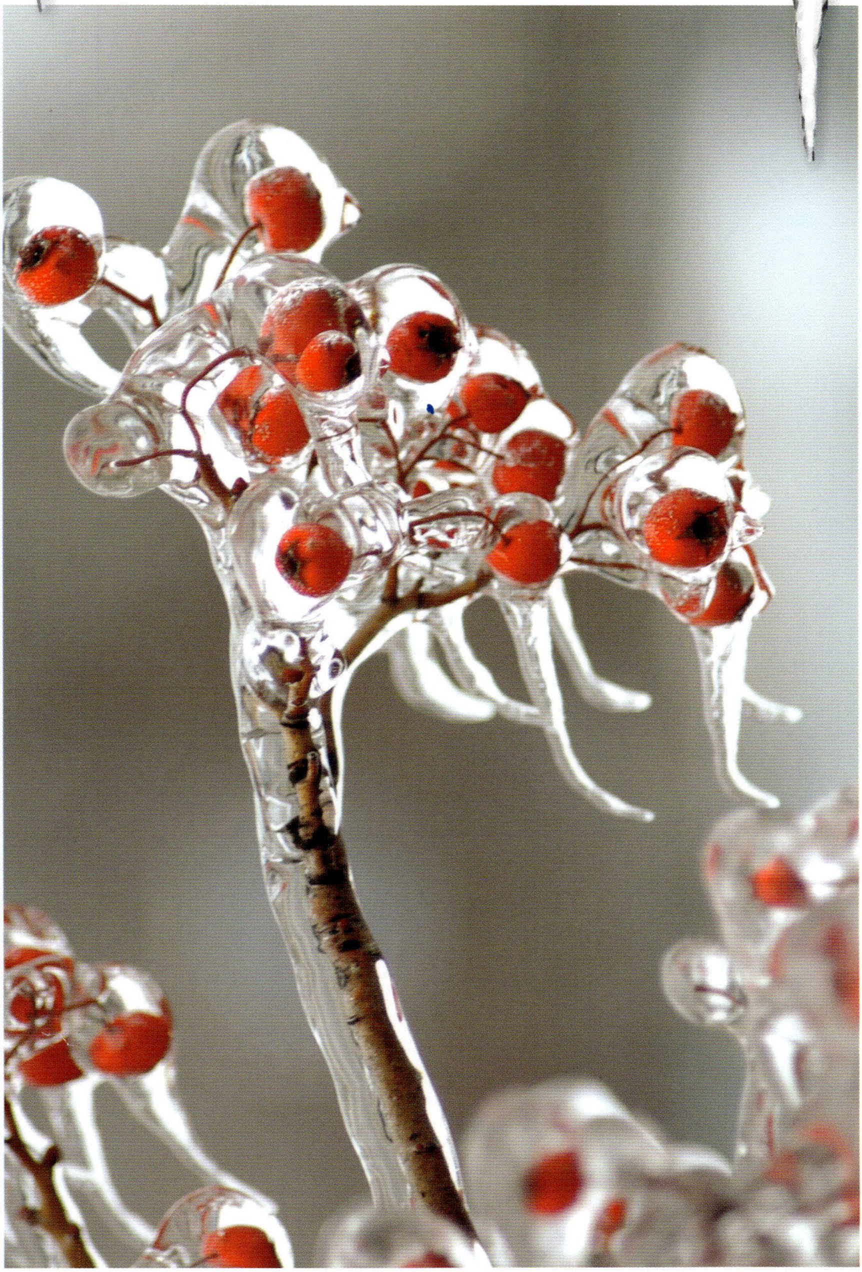

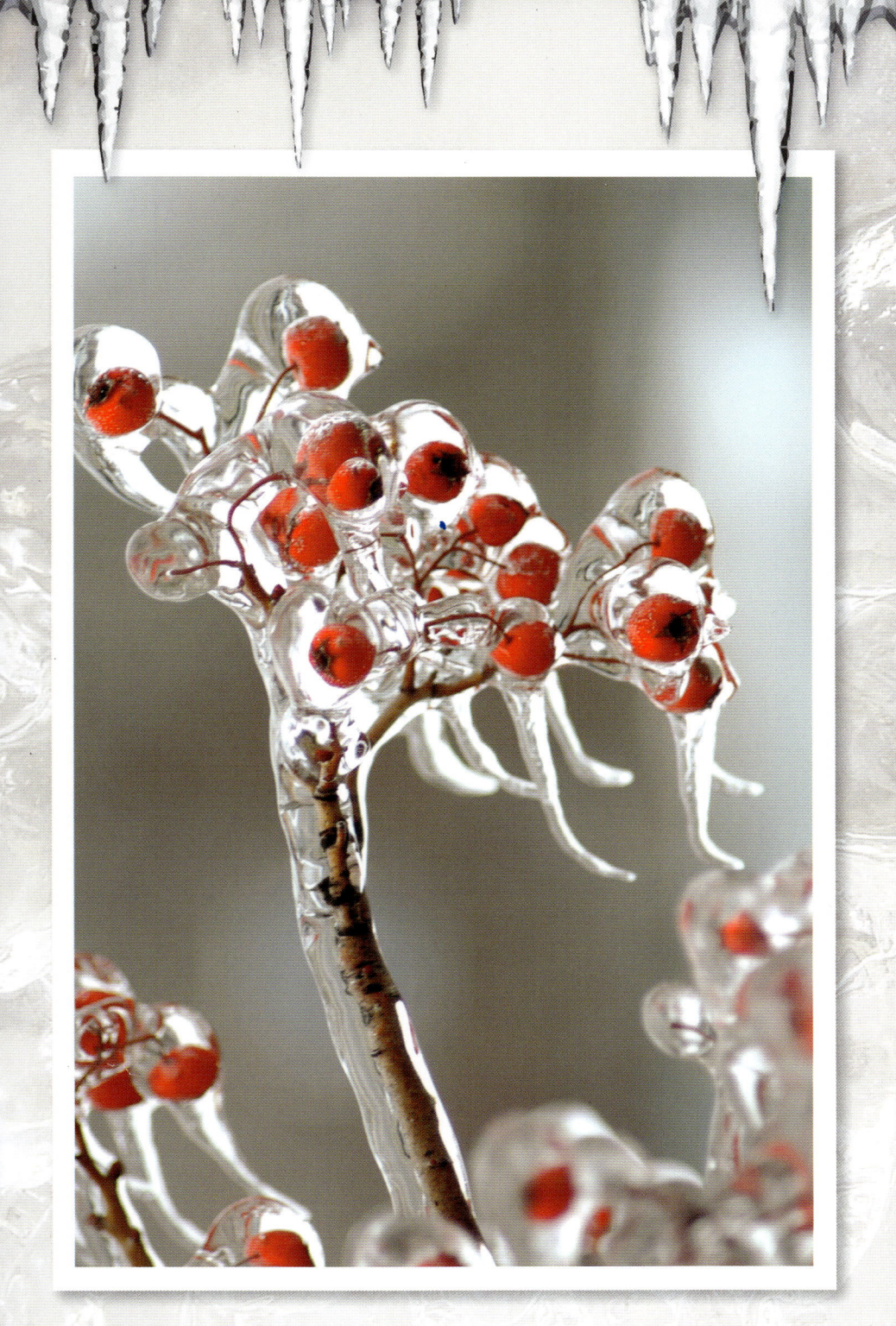

There is ice on the fence.

13

There is ice on the sign.

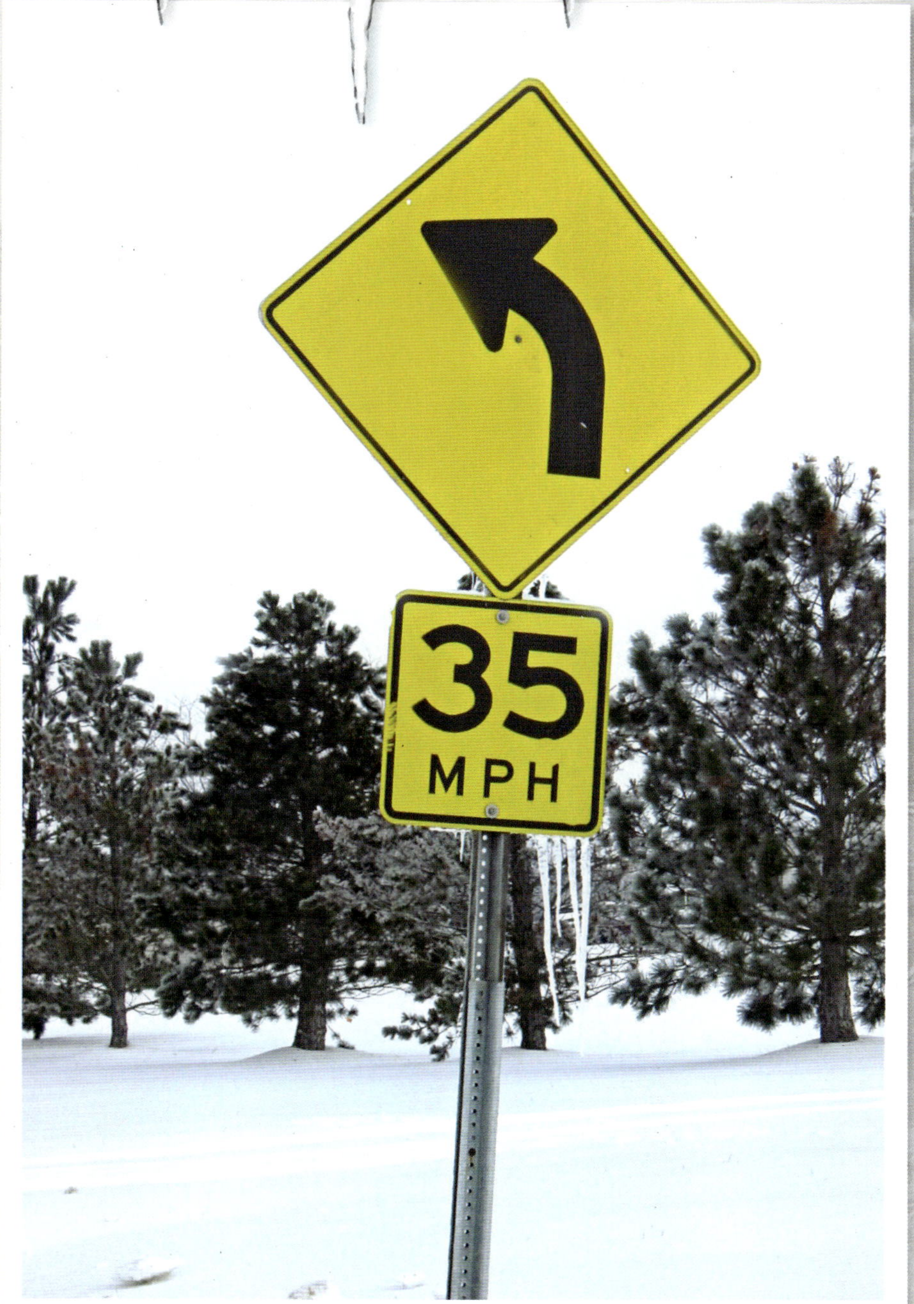
35
MPH

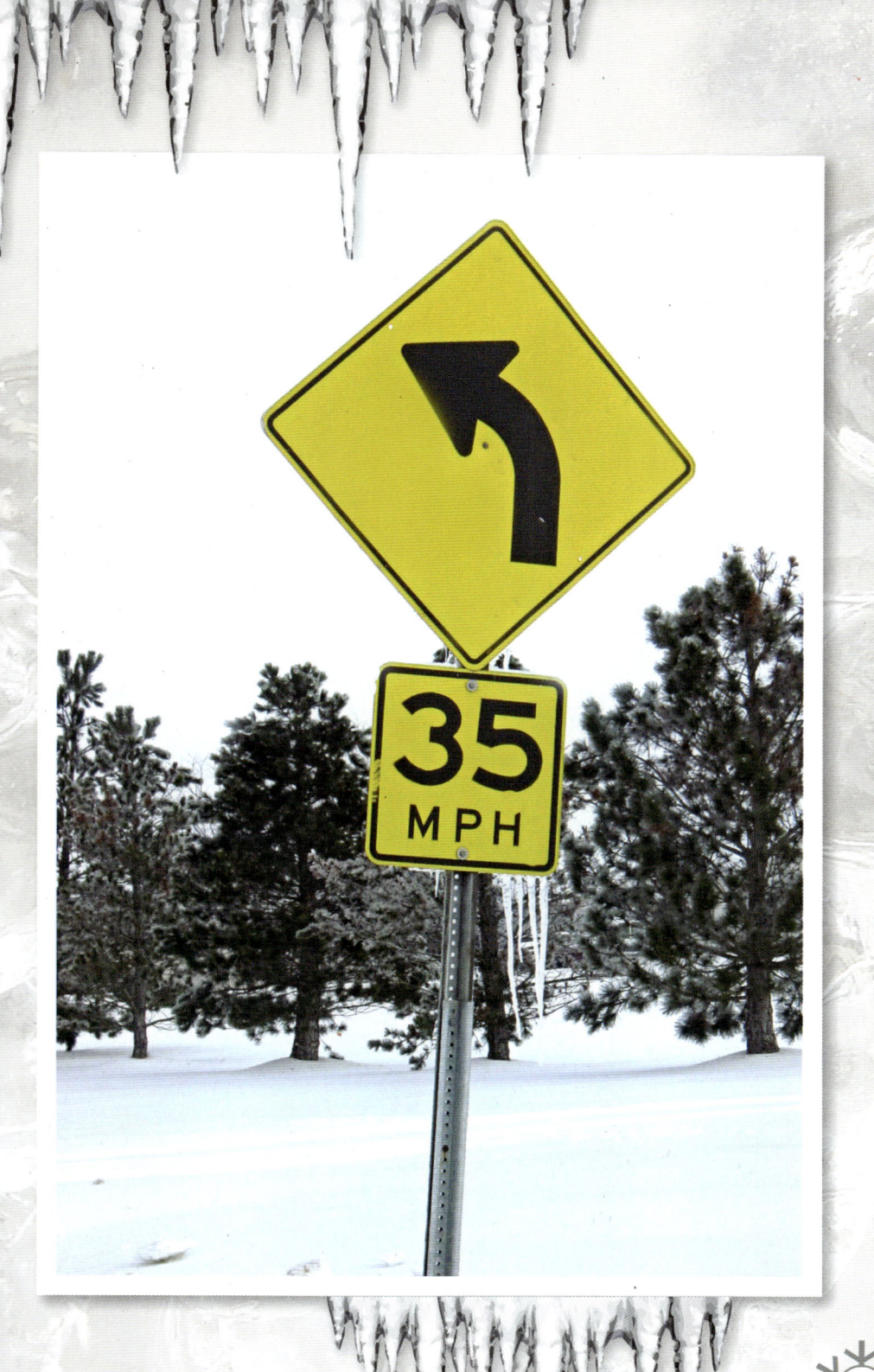

There is ice on the bench.

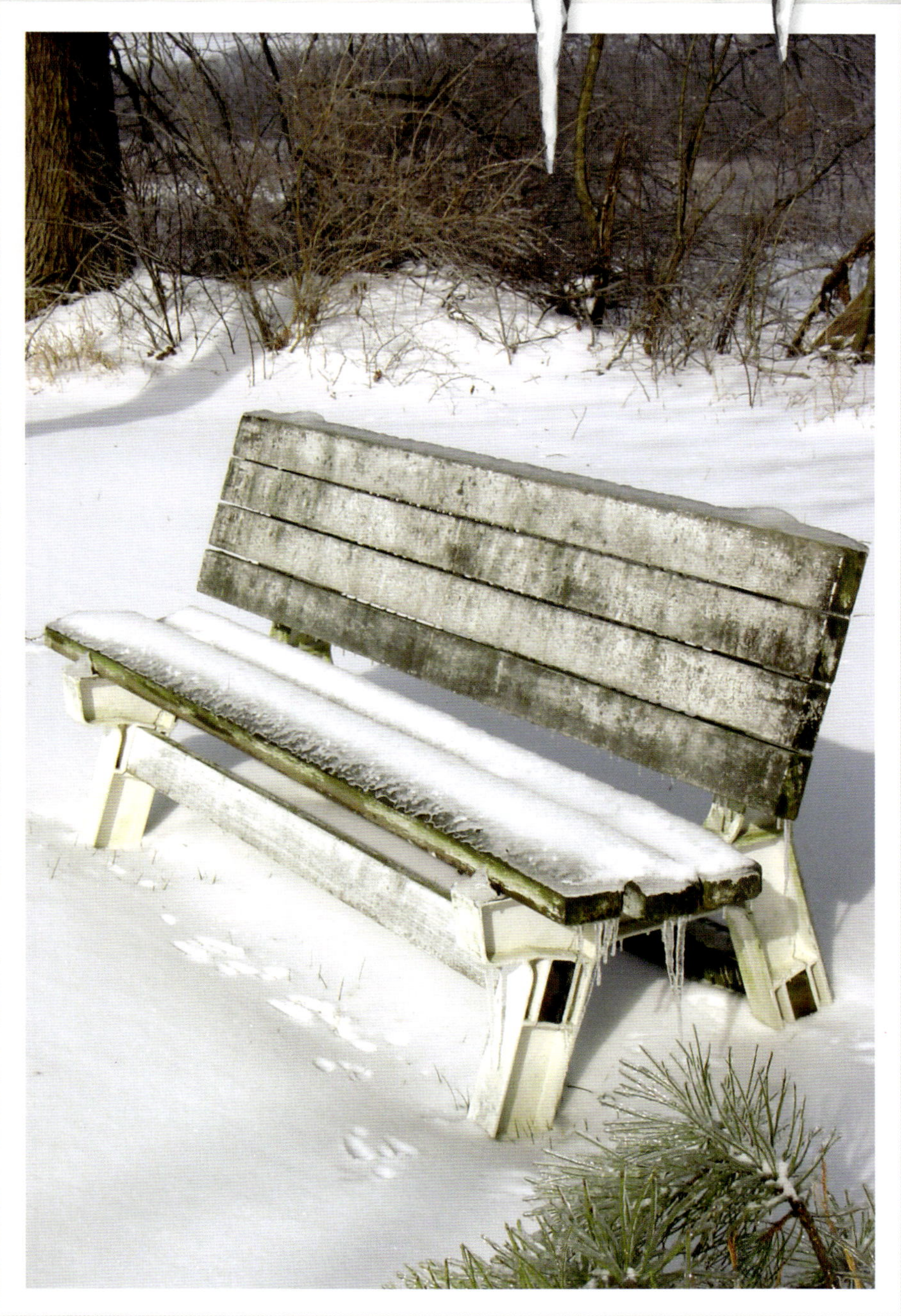

# 1-3Y: Skills Card

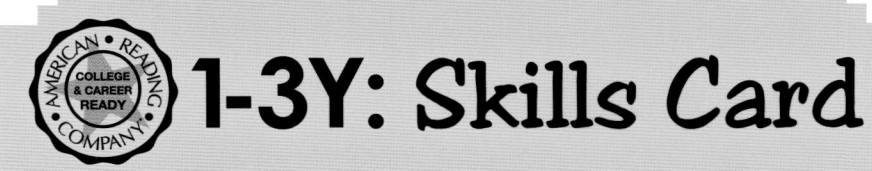

Reader: _____   Room: _____

| "What was this book mainly about? How do you know?" |
|---|

| 1Y | Listen to and remember the sentence pattern in Yellow books. Use the pattern and pictures to read the rest of the book. |
|---|---|
| 2Y | Point to each word as I read. Use the spaces to separate words. |
|  | Try again if what I say doesn't match the number of words. |
| 3Y | Make the sound of the first letter of the new word on the page, check the picture, then say something that matches both. |

**I can get my mouth ready for:**

| b | c | d |
|---|---|---|
| f | g | h |
| j | k | l |
| m | n | p |
| r | s | t |
| v | w | z |

Copyright © 2010 by American Reading Company®

**I can use the first letter sound to match the word to the picture.**

steps

fence

berries

tree

# Power Words

## How many can you read?

There

there

is

on

the